Asli's Story

Adrienne Jansen

Learning Media

Contents

*I*magine this. Your peaceful home isn't peaceful anymore. Armed men patrol the streets every day. At night, you see the red flare of bullets exploding in the air. Your family want to go somewhere that is safer, but the gunmen control the streets, and you can't get out of your neighborhood. Your father has to give them money before they will let you all travel to the center of the city. But you can't take anything with you, not even a small bag, or the gunmen will know that you are escaping, and there will be trouble. So you leave your country and the home that you love and travel great distances looking for a safe country that will let you stay. You are a refugee.

This is the story of twelve-year-old Asli Mohamed Abdulaziz Mohamed, who is a refugee. Her story begins in Somalia, where she was born, and ends in a country thousands of miles away.

1. Asli's Family

Asli comes from Somalia. Her family home was in the capital city, Mogadishu, a modern city of 700,000 people, where her father worked as an accountant. Asli's family lived in a three-storied house. It had ten rooms and three bathrooms, a separate TV and video room, and a large open living area on the roof. There was only one other building on their block, and that was the U.S. **embassy**.

Somalia

Somalia is sometimes called the "number seven country" because of its shape.

- Population: 7,555,000
- Area: 246,000 square miles (slightly smaller than Texas)
- Capital: Mogadishu
- Languages: Somali, Arabic, Italian, English
- Main crops: bananas, sugar, **sorghum**, corn
- Religion: Sunni Muslim

The Benadir

If you ask Asli where she's from, she'll say that she's from Somalia, but she is not a Somali. Her family are Benadir.

The Benadir are a group of people who came to Somalia from Arabia about a thousand years ago. Somalis are traditionally **nomadic** people, but the Benadir mostly live in cities. They are peaceful people who value education and business. They are of the Muslim faith. Since the war began, the Benadir community has been scattered around the world, with many living in the United States. There is only a small number of Benadir people still living in Somalia today.

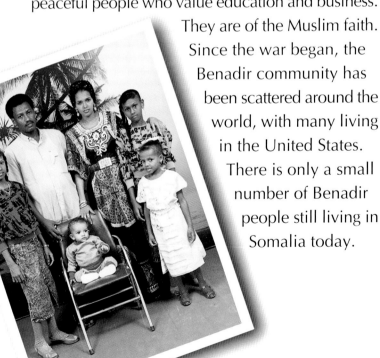

Asli was born in 1987 in Merka, a town on the Somali coast, where her grandparents lived. At that time, Mogadishu was becoming a dangerous place, with fighting breaking out between different **clans** that wanted to control the country. Asli's parents decided that it would be safer for her to stay in Merka with her grandparents.

Right: Asli as a toddler (left) with her aunts and sister

Below: Asli (middle) with her sisters

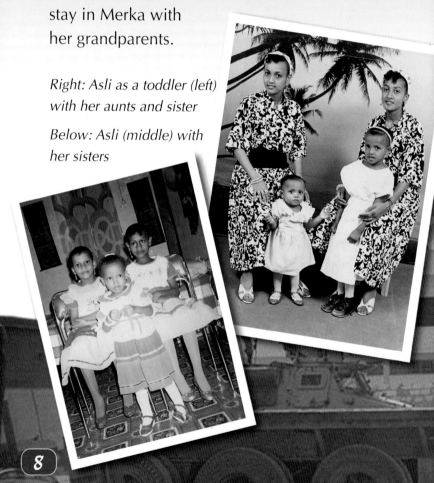

2. The War in Somalia

In 1988, when Asli was one year old, the fighting in Somalia grew into a **civil war**.

The government collapsed – no one was making laws or enforcing them anymore, and many schools and hospitals were destroyed. Somalia became a very violent and dangerous place. People weren't safe even in their own homes, and many people were killed every day. Thousands more died of starvation because the farms and factories couldn't operate normally, and severe **droughts** made the situation worse.

Life in Somalia became very difficult. Whenever Asli's father left the house, he would tell the family, "If I don't come back, you'll know I am dead." Asli's parents visited her in Merka as often as they could, but the trip from Mogadishu was very dangerous. On the seventy-mile journey, they had to pass twenty roadblocks. At each one, her father had to give money to the armed guards before he could go through.

About 400,000 people died in the fighting in Somalia at this time, and about a million others fled from the fighting and the hunger. They became **refugees**, looking for new lives in other countries. By the time Asli was four, her parents had decided to leave Somalia too.

Leaving Somalia

Getting out of Somalia was very difficult for Asli's family. They wanted to go to Kenya, but all the boats going there were full. Finally, after two months of waiting, they managed to get places on a small boat. For six days, the family were crammed together with about 160 people while the boat sailed down the Somali coast to Mombasa in Kenya.

It was a terrible trip. The sea was very rough, and most people were sick. There was only one toilet. The sun was burning hot, and there was little shade.

When Asli and her family first arrived in Mombasa, they lived in an old school and later with other families in a village outside the city. Then they finally went to live in a camp that was set up especially for Benadir refugees. They stayed there for four and a half years.

3. The Refugee Camp

*O*ver 4,000 people were living in the camp. Asli and her family shared two small huts built out of a kind of bamboo. These huts had sandy floors with lots of tiny insects living in the sand that burrowed into their hands and feet. There was food, supplied by the **Red Cross**, and water from wells in the camp – but never enough of either. It was a hard time.

Although they were living in a refugee camp, Asli's parents wanted their children to have a good education. But there are nine children in Asli's family, and schooling costs a lot in Kenya, so only three of the children went to school. Asli and her other brothers and sisters spent the mornings playing in the camp playground or helping their parents. Every afternoon, they went to the **mosque**, where they learned to read and write in Arabic and to read the **Koran**.

The main thing Asli remembers about that camp was the toilets. "They were outside and always messy, and there were long queues. And there were mice. My brother chased the mice, then my father came and killed them."

On the Move

Then the Kenyan Government decided to move all the refugee camps north to a place called Kakuma. It was a hard move. The Benadir community were split up among different camps – even families were separated. Asli's family lost contact with some of her aunts and uncles.

Asli's family were about to move to the new camp when they got some good news. Asli's half-brother, who lived in New Zealand, had successfully applied to the New Zealand Government for the family to go and live in New Zealand.

Nairobi, Kenya

Wellington, New Zealand

So in 1997, instead of moving to the Kakuma camp, they flew out to begin a new and totally different life in Wellington, the capital city of New Zealand.

4. A Different World

Asli and her family arrived in Wellington in the middle of winter. Imagine what it must have been like, coming from a hot, dry country to a cold, wet, windy one! Their new life was very difficult at first. Everything, not just the weather, was different from what they were used to – the language, food, clothes, and customs.

Asli was ten when she arrived in her new country. She had never been to school before, and suddenly she had to go every day. It seemed very strange to her that boys and girls worked together in the same classroom and played together in the schoolyard. In Somalia, as in other Muslim countries, boys and girls are strictly separated for most activities.

At school, Asli was surrounded by the English language. She could understand a little of what the teacher said, but she couldn't reply in English. And she couldn't understand the other children's talk at all.

Fortunately, she wasn't on her own at school. Five members of her family started school together, along with five children from another Somali family. It was a big help to Asli having other Somali people there to explain things to her in her own language. A teacher gave the group special help in math and English, too.

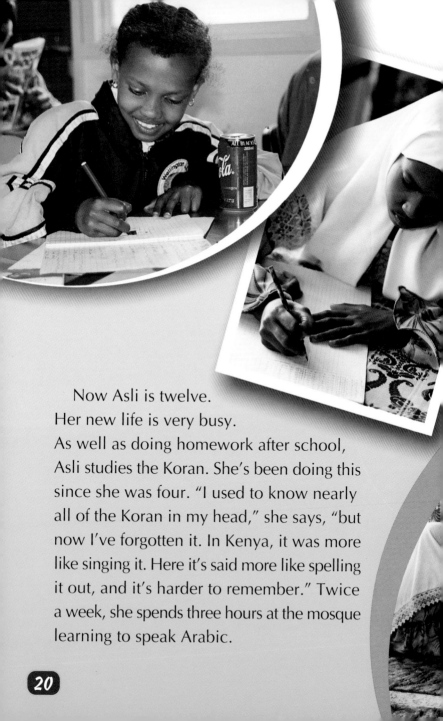

Now Asli is twelve.
Her new life is very busy.
As well as doing homework after school,
Asli studies the Koran. She's been doing this
since she was four. "I used to know nearly
all of the Koran in my head," she says, "but
now I've forgotten it. In Kenya, it was more
like singing it. Here it's said more like spelling
it out, and it's harder to remember." Twice
a week, she spends three hours at the mosque
learning to speak Arabic.

Many things that were part of life in Somalia don't happen here, such as storytelling. In Somalia, the oldest woman of the family calls all the children around her, and they all sit together on the ground as she tells them the ancient stories of their culture. But in Asli's new country, everyone watches TV instead.

There's always someone at home in a Somali household. Families are large – usually with eight or nine children, like Asli's – and often include the extended family, such as grandparents and uncles and aunts. In Asli's new country, the family is just her parents and her brothers and sisters. Her family finds it very difficult not having all of their relatives around them. They still don't even know where many of them are. But they are hoping to find them with the help of the Red Cross, which works with families to find missing relatives all over the world.

New Friends

What's it like to wear clothes that are different from everyone else's, speak a different language, and even play different games?

Sometimes Asli is teased because of her clothes. When they are in public, Benadir Muslim women and girls cover their heads with a hijab, or scarf, and keep their bodies covered. Some of Asli's classmates misunderstand this Muslim custom.

One boy thought that they hide their hair because if they show it, he said, "The police will do something to them." But another one who understands better said, "They cover their heads for their religion."

There are days when Asli doesn't bring any lunch or snacks to school. This is during the month of **Ramadan**, when Muslims **fast** – adults don't eat at all between sunrise and sunset. Asli fasts only every second day. She doesn't find it difficult not being able to eat at lunchtime when everyone else is eating because it's what she has known all her life. But some of her classmates think that it's weird.

Asli's classmates know that she comes from Somalia and that Somalia's in Africa, but they don't know much about the country or its people. If you ask them about Somalia, they say things like:

"People live in mud houses or little tents."

"People live on the streets – except there aren't any streets."

"They don't have technology, they don't have TV, and they don't wear T-shirts."

"The men work to gather food or chop wood. The children go to work when they're four years old, and they do work like bringing water from the creek."

Some of these things are true for some people in Somalia – many Somali people are extremely poor and struggle to stay alive. But Asli's life has not been like that. She wishes that her classmates would ask her about her home in Somalia because then they would understand her – and Somalia – better.

Today the war in Somalia is still going on. The clans are still fighting for power, and peace is a long way off. Asli's family would like to go back to Somalia some day, but they don't know when that will be. For now, her family is settled in their new country.

Timeline

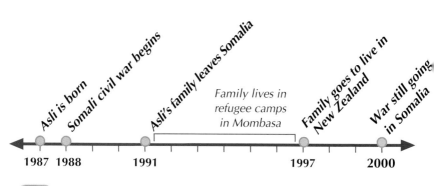

Asli is born

Somali civil war begins

Asli's family leaves Somalia

Family lives in refugee camps in Mombasa

Family goes to live in New Zealand

War still going in Somalia

1987 1988 1991 1997 2000

Glossary

(These words are printed in bold type the first time they appear in the book.)

civil war: a war between different groups in one country

clan: a large group of people who have a common ancestor

drought: a long period of extremely dry weather

embassy: the official offices of one country that are based in another country

fast: to stop eating for a short time for health or religious reasons

Koran: the Muslim book of holy scripture

mosque: a Muslim place of worship

nomadic: having a wandering way of life without a permanent home

Ramadan: the ninth month of the Muslim calendar

Red Cross: an international aid organization

refugee: a person who flees their country because of war or political unrest

sorghum: a cereal crop

Index